Foreword

I am convinced this little book is a masterpiece. It contains much-needed wisdom in an (apparently) very simple form; the simplicity encompassing rich teachings about emotional and spiritual literacy.

Although on the surface a book for children, there is much here of value to their parents, teachers and caregivers.

Recent British governments (of both political persuasions) seem increasingly reluctant to trust children's natural learning processes, or a spontaneous engagement by their teachers based on this. The ideas in this book are the polar opposite of 'control from above' – the parents, teachers and caregivers are encouraged to find that perfect balance where they are facilitating, but not controlling, the education that unfolds.

There is a beautiful combination in this book: the wisdom underlying Nicola's text is complemented perfectly by Beatrix-Renata Bihari's charming pictures. The ideas in this book are deceptively simple – but as a psychologist they convey to me profound messages about growth, boundaries, assertiveness, and emotional literacy. The great skill shown here is that Nicola translates this emotional intelligence into a form even young children can engage with. To say the least, that is not an easy thing to do, and I congratulate Nicola on how very well she has achieved it.

Any child encountering this book is fortunate indeed.

Dr Martin Treacy M.A. (Oxon) PhD CSci C.Psychol AFBPsS

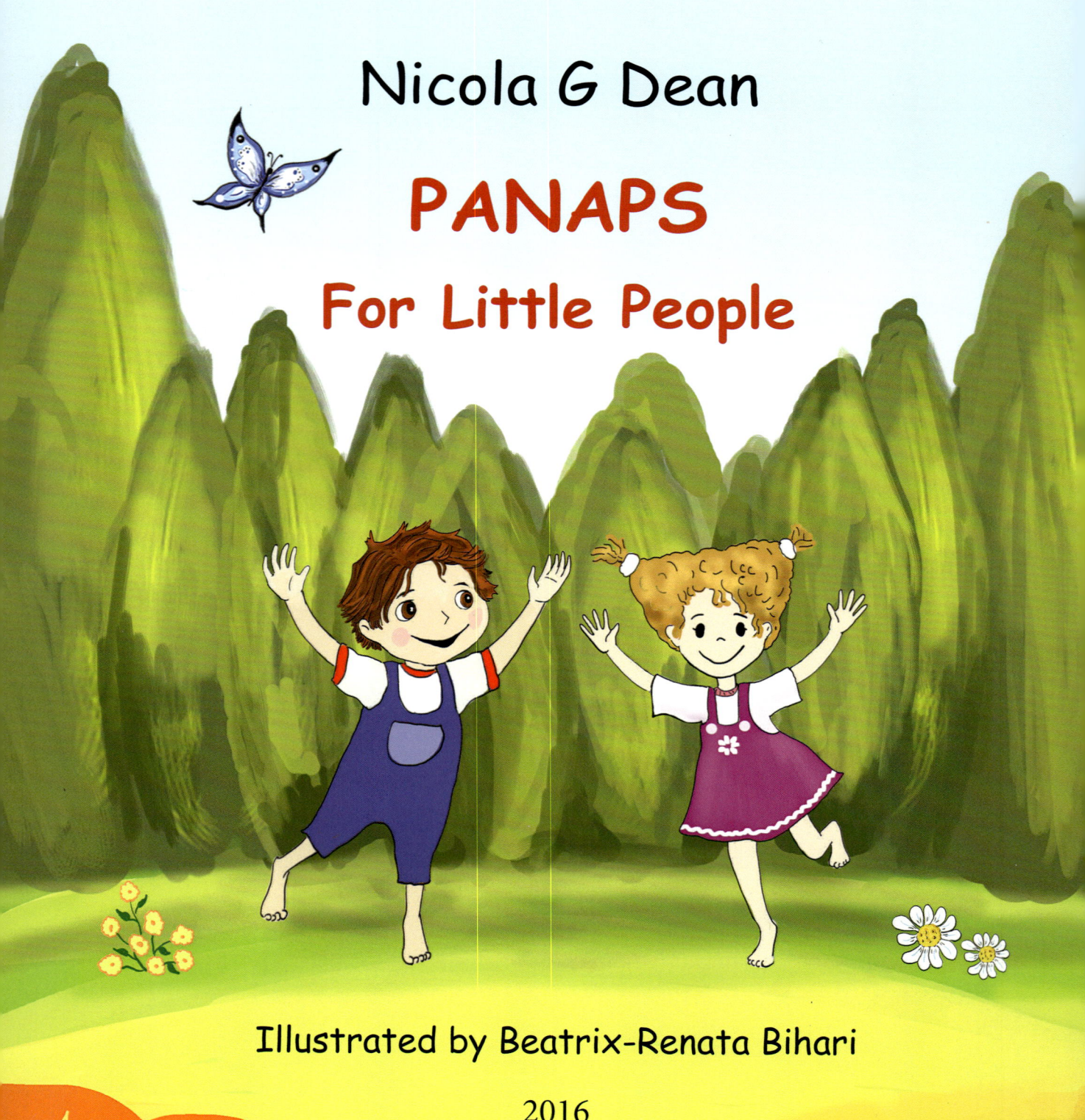

Contents

Learning to Write with Patience   4

Pure Fun and Silliness   8

Beat your Bully   12

Saying Sorry   20

Boundaries   24

No More 'Ought To's'   28

Learning to Write with Patience

That's it, draw a line,
As straight as it can be.
I'll do it first for you
And then you copy me.

Hold the pen firmly,
Closer to the tip.
Press a little harder, but...
Without too much grip.

Follow the lines, Mum tells him,
The circle and the square.
I'm trying, Mum, stop shouting,
You're not being fair.

I'm doing my best, Jack snaps back,
I want it as good as can be.
I promise, Mum, I'd love it
If I could write my name - you'll see.

Sorry son, I had forgotten
How long it took me to learn.
I'll be patient, try and help you,
Please have another turn.

So Mum writes 'Jack' on the paper
And gives him back the pen.
They have a renewed patience,
And work together again.

The Importance Of Patience

Without the unsaid pressure
And expectation from his mum.
A new career in writing
J - A - C - K - has just begun.

- We grown-ups sometimes forget what it's like to be little. Be patient.
- Ask them why it feels nicer when people are patient.

Pure Fun and Silliness

Make cakes and lick the bowl,
Play in the garden and handle coal.
Tell jokes, laugh, and tickle each other.
Take a torch under the duvet cover.

Make up silly rhymes and climb trees,
Play piggy backs on your knees.
Hide and seek, painting, fighting and fun;
The list of free fun has just begun.

Paint the soles of your feet
And walk on paper laid down.
Eat marshmallows and chocolate
And dress up as a clown.

Play guessing games and collecting things.
That's it, your mind's ticking over.
Pretend you're a bird and spread your wings.
Look for a four-leaf clover.

Lie in the garden on a starry night,
Plant seeds and grow a sunflower.
Go out when it's windy and fly a kite,
Measure the height - 'as big as a tower'.

Listen to the music
And guess who sang the song.
It's important to create togetherness
For a whole day long.

Fun Time To Talk

Your sense of closeness is growing,
You're feeling chuffed with your day.
Let's do this again some time,
Will be the first thing you'll say.

You may not have much money,
But you've got fun times in your heart.
The togetherness will make you happy
And that's a really good start.

- Ask the child what 'free fun' ideas they have.
- Plan to do 'free fun' activities and pay attention to how everyone feels.

Beat your Bully

Little Jim was quiet
When he came home from school.
He had a hard day
Being bullied and treated cruel.

He couldn't tell his mother
'Cause Davie would call him thick.
Tease him worse than yesterday.
So Jim told his mum 'I'm sick'.

It was easier to get attention
Without the truth being shared,
'Cause the bully had already told him
Tell your mum and you'll be scared.

Little Jim was crying
And said his tummy ached.
It's a regular story by victims
And one that's usually faked.

But Jim's Mum pushed
And asked what's wrong.
Come on, Mummy's little Jim,
This has been going on too long.

Jim broke down in tears, and said,
'You promise not to tell?'
But at the last minute he backed out
Saying his arm hurt because he fell.

His mum knew something wasn't right,
Both knew he didn't fall.
So the bullying had to be sorted out,
Once, and for all.

It's always a pressure when you're scared
But Davie was causing the trouble.
It's hard to rise above it
When teased about your 'Mummy's cuddle'.

Jim's mum said if you're being picked on,
The bully's the one who's scared.
Jim burst into tears and said he's not, Mum,
He's tough and ginger haired.

What is it he says to you,
Let's understand his jeers.
He says he thinks I'm stupid
And that I've got big ears.

Do you think you're stupid, Jim?
No, I get all A's and B's.
And what grades does that boy Davie get -
I bet it's C's and D's.

You are right, Mum,
But how could you tell?
He's picking on you
'cause he's not doing well.

Let's put a stop to it
And stand up tall.
Don't tell me you've got a tummy ache
And had a fall

I love you, Jim, you've got lots of friends,
I bet Davie's jealous of you.
We'll make a stand together
We know what to do.

So let's just go,
Find out what's wrong.
Come on, little Jimmy,
You're just as big and strong.

Encouraging Truth

• Children can tell little fibs when they are bullied because they don't know how to deal with what they're facing.

We'll tell your friends so they keep an eye
And the teachers, so they know too.
If we put a stop to it now,
He won't do it to someone new.

So you'll be helping someone else
From feeling just as low.
Come on - coat on, shoes on,
It's time for us to go.

Ok Mum,
Says Jim with a frown,
I'll show Bully Davies
I'm not a clown!

- Encouraging truth from a child will help them feel looked after as you are showing an interest in how they really feel.
- Listening 'care-fully' is very important. When you listen to them they feel they are worth listening to. This gives them self-esteem and the strength to be honest.

Saying Sorry

I woke up this morning,
Feeling very glum.
So I got out of bed
And I looked for my mum.

I was horrid when I saw her,
I frowned, shouted and glared.
Mum didn't find that nice,
So she yelled back, and I got scared.

I cried, and stomped back out,
And she ranted as I walked.
Oh, I wish I'd given her a cuddle,
Been nice, and we had talked.

The damage has been done anyway,
I feel worse than I did.
Now my mum feels terrible,
'cause I was a horrid kid.

I sit on my bed, and think for a while
And realise what I've done.
I want to make it better
So I say sorry to my mum.

Self-Reflection

We hug, and start again,
The way it should have been.
Tomorrow when I wake up,
I will not be so mean.

As all this time's been wasted,
With a bad feeling in the air.
There was no point in it at all,
So we cuddle now, and care.

- Encourage the child to think about a time when they could have made a sad situation happier.

Boundaries

Have a talk about boundaries, rules
And what it is they're for.
Explain the reasons behind them
And pin them on the door.

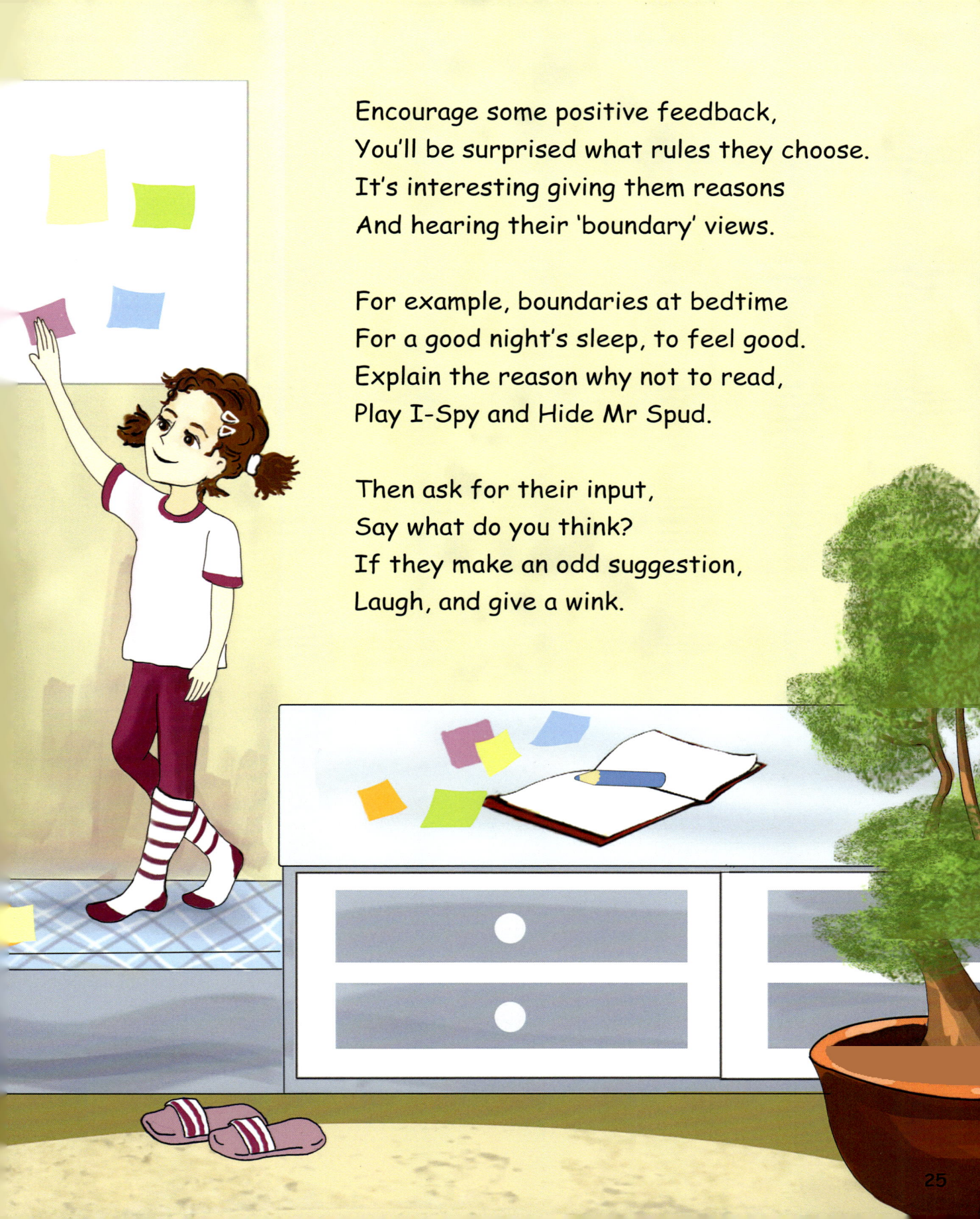

Encourage some positive feedback,
You'll be surprised what rules they choose.
It's interesting giving them reasons
And hearing their 'boundary' views.

For example, boundaries at bedtime
For a good night's sleep, to feel good.
Explain the reason why not to read,
Play I-Spy and Hide Mr Spud.

Then ask for their input,
Say what do you think?
If they make an odd suggestion,
Laugh, and give a wink.

Say, come on now, a grown-up chat,
But nothing very deep.
Ask them why they think there are
Rules about going to sleep.

If they give the answer,
Which often is the case.
You'll be building an understanding
That your child can face.

Boundaries Chat
- If they are set in the right way they build love and trust, and make children feel safe.

Talk about different boundaries,
Like crossing a busy road.
Help with your child's understanding
With stories like Dad and Son Toad.

Give your child the freedom
And let him show his skill.
He knows more than you would think,
Ask a question and answer he will.

- Ask the child why he or she thinks boundaries / rules are important. You will be creating respect by showing them you are interested in hearing what they have to say.

No More 'Ought To's'

I don't want to go to their house,
I'll be naughty as can be.
"Come on, you'll be fine, you ought to...
We have to go and have tea".

Oh, no, it's obvious,
Even I can see,
Mum and Dad don't want to go,
It's not just me!

Because they say we ought to,
Which means THEY really must.
Out of pressure or expectation -
I'm young, but I've got it sussed.

So, tell me, why do we have to go,
If no-one's feeling nice.
Why don't we cut the times down,
From five times a week to twice?

Then we won't feel so resentful,
And Gran won't pick up how we feel.
We could go there because we wanted to,
And eat and enjoy the meal.

Why are we caught up with 'ought to's'?
They seem to rule our life.
I can see it 'cause I'm little -
Not bogged down in adult strife

But it's only how you make it,
It's open to interpretation.
Less pressure, and happiness
That's a cause for celebration.

So let's phone up and just be nice,
Say we won't be coming today.
We'll come again in a few days' time
And have lunch - what do you say?

That will be great, says Grandma,
I can potter as I'd been.
It'll be nice to have a few days' break,
I know just what you mean.

'Ought To's'

It turns out Gran's been wanting her space,
But didn't like to say.
We've been going 'cause we 'ought to',
Nearly every day.

So now we're all contented,
I can go and play.
Not worry about the 'ought to's'
For another day.

• Ask the child if they understand the idea of 'should's' and 'ought to's'.
Get them to give you some examples.

Acknowledgments:

I would like to share my heartfelt appreciation for the following who have supported me in producing this book.

Illustrator - Beatrix-Renata Bihari
Editor - Jackie Hadley
Publisher - Sarah Banfield
Printer - Lewis Printers, Carmarthen
Foreword - Dr Martin Treacy
Kay Mondon and Charlie John for such lovely reviews

Johnny Farkas - Hungarian translator, without his help the illustrator and I would have struggled to iron out some of the finer detail.

Friends and family who have encouraged me and supported me practically and financially over six years to bring these out from under the bed and get them through the process and into the world.

Copyright © Nicola G Dean

All rights reserved. No part of this book may be reproduced or transmitted in any form or by any means, electronic or mechanical, including photocopying or recording, or by any information storage and retrieval system, without permission in writing from the author, except in the case of brief quotations embodied in reviews.

Story by Nicola G Dean
nicoladean.com
https://www.facebook.com/panapsbook

Book Illustrations by Beatrix-Renata Bihari
Edited by Jackie Hadley

Sakayi Publishing
Sarah Kay Banfield
25 Eversfield Place
St Leonards on Sea. TN37 6BY

ISBN 978-0-9551902-7-8